I WILL BE
CORRUPTED

ESSENTIAL POETS SERIES 271

**Canada Council
for the Arts**

**Conseil des Arts
du Canada**

**ONTARIO ARTS COUNCIL
CONSEIL DES ARTS DE L'ONTARIO**

an Ontario government agency
un organisme du gouvernement de l'Ont

Canadä

Guernica Editions Inc. acknowledges the support of the Canada Council
for the Arts and the Ontario Arts Council. The Ontario Arts Council
is an agency of the Government of Ontario.

We acknowledge the financial support of the Government of Canada.

JOSEPH A. DANDURAND

I WILL BE CORRUPTED

**GUERNICA
EDITIONS**

TORONTO – CHICAGO – BUFFALO – LANCASTER (U.K.)
2020

Michael Mirolla, editor
Cover and interior design: Errol F. Richardson
Cover image: Errol F. Richardson
Guernica Editions Inc.
287 Templemead Drive, Hamilton, (ON), Canada L8W 2W4
2250 Military Road, Tonawanda, N.Y. 14150-6000 U.S.A.
www.guernicaeditions.com

Distributors:
Independent Publishers Group (IPG)
600 North Pulaski Road, Chicago IL 60624
University of Toronto Press Distribution,
5201 Dufferin Street, Toronto (ON), Canada M3H 5T8
Gazelle Book Services, White Cross Mills
High Town, Lancaster LA1 4XS U.K.

First edition.
Printed in Canada.

Legal Deposit – Third Quarter
Library of Congress Catalog Card Number: 2019949196
Library and Archives Canada Cataloguing in Publication
Title: I will be corrupted / Joseph A. Dandurand.
Names: Dandurand, Joseph A., author.
Series: Essential poets ; 271.
Description: Series statement: Essential poets series ; 271
Identifiers: Canadiana 2019017420X | ISBN 9781771835060 (softcover)
Classification: LCC PS8557.A523 I2 2020 | DDC C811/.54—dc21

*To my Mother Josette who survived
so I too could also survive*

CONTENTS

That which binds

if they ever found
out what it is
that I have done
in this life they
would surely
call it: a waste.

wake up and light a
smoke and reheat a
cold coffee from yesterday
and let the dog out and watched
the sun come out of the
mist of a May morning
here on this island.

the village awaits the
great flood but it
never comes and we
sit here and beg for
the snow to melt in
the mountains up river
and the snow melts and
the river's edge comes
to us in a carpet of
destruction and we
await the fish
to come
and they do in millions
and we attack them
with our nets and we
take as much as we can
and we await

the rains of fall
and they come
and the world we know
slows on this island
and we await that which
binds us here forever
and our people
the last of a tribe
await the funeral
that awaits all of us
here on this island
that is too far from
the mountain's snow
that melts
over and over
and that is
what binds
us
to
this
existence.

Though disturbed

the walk from here to
there is never quite
what I had in mind
when I was a young man.

so the steps now at 50
are very carefully taken
one two three and watch
out not to stumble
in front of my kids.

I used to jump and leap
over fences and took all
the boundaries down
as I glided to and fro
into another mysterious
love affair.

there she was on a cloud
of love for her and I
as we took off all our
clothes and melted in
the bliss of the forgotten
and we never even came up
for air and we died in
each other's arms
and when they found us
they said the word: empty.

this is where I am on
the third day of a deep
depression and I and I eat
very little as the sun beats
us all up a little and
there are no clouds to
shade my shame of who
I am but the words
fly out of me and empty
to the page and though
disturbed by my image
and I walk slowly
into the fourth day
of my depression
and the world stumbles
behind me trying to
take me further away
to the place
called: empty.

Deep in the corner of my eye

when I think about it
I woke up fighting and
my first fight was at
the age of four
and some older boys beat me
up and so I waited for them
to get off the school bus and
I just swung that hockey stick
until the slivers in my hands
allowed me to drop my
weapon of choice and from
that day forward they
showed me
mercy.

today I fight the demons
in my mind who show
up from time to time
and they breathe on
my neck to remind me
that all is not working
for me so I walk into
the river and I dunk
myself four times and
under the water I swing
that hockey stick
until the slivers of my
mind float down river
to the ocean and then
I step out of the water
and all the demons retreat
into the trees and on the

tallest tree sits an eagle
who whistles to me
and in the deep corner
of my eye I see the words
forming in a silhouette
of forgiveness
and the
word
I see
is
mercy.

Desire that carved me

once I sat down and had
tea with a sasquatch
and he said he had seen
all the mountains on earth
and I believed him as
he sipped his tea and stared
off across the valley to the
snow-capped mountains above.

later I met up with an owl
who said she had seen death
and the other side where all
our dear ones were still
hungry and wished for
more smoked fish and
potato chips and the owl
took off into the night
and climbed as high as the
moon as the smell of
smoked fish and potato chips
filled the air.

fishing on the river a
sturgeon came to my boat
and she told me she had
found a body on the bottom
of a friend of mine from
up river and that he was ok
but now rested in one of
the deepest fishing holes
on the river and the sturgeon
slowly fell to the bottom

and began to feed on my
friend from up river and all
was so quiet as the sounds
of the sucking lips of the
sturgeon echoed down river.

when I went to sleep
a spirit came to me and said
it is time and we shared a
laugh of how I had lived
so long and the spirit
left out the window
and whispered to me that
I will one day find love
and so I closed my eyes
and my dream
was that
of the desire
that
carved
me.

I did not gather

we are all here for the
same reason or another
and the breaths we take in
and out and in and out
give us the time to
experience all that life
has given us and we
never question our place here
and I am like that in some way
as I guide my people
away from despair.

we are all the same and our
hearts beat for decades and
decades and we grow old and
slow a bit and eat very little
and we do not become great
beings of strength and wisdom
but we become the lost shells
on the beach of eternity.

we are all alone on a planet
filled with lost and forgotten
people who may live to
starve to death and they may
live to die in a fire set by a
madman but we move on
and we breathe the poisonous
air into the unattractive one
thousandth day of our lives.

we are all sinners
of one religion or another
and if I could find my angel
I would make love to her
and we would have children
who would drown in the
lust of all the other evil
men who wander this earth
and only appear when they
are caught in the
spider's web.

we are all told at birth
that one day you will
vanish and I did not
gather that idea of
living forever and so
I find myself being reborn
and reborn and reincarnated
as a simple man with four walls
and a doorway and one window
overlooking the rising river of
my love for all that
breathes
in and out
and in
and
out.

At night I am broken again

I have tried and failed
at taking my own life and the
first time I ran out into
oncoming traffic and I was
broken up and drunk and did
not realize that the girl I loved
did not even know who I was.

spent some time in a madhouse
and slept beside Jesus and he
woke me up one night and told
me to drink his blood and eat
the body of Christ and I did
because he was Jesus and you
do not deny Christ even when
he began to sing songs of glory.

I had a dream of driving my car
into oncoming traffic but my mind
could not trick my arms from pulling
the trigger so I drove
from coast to coast smoking
cigarettes and drinking whiskey.

I've slit my wrists but only
deep enough to draw blood
and I watch it drip to the ground
and form a puddle around my
bare feet and I began to dance
in a circle and beg forgiveness
as the sirens could be heard
in the distance racing to me
as I slowly bled.

I imagined hanging myself
in my smokehouse at the
back of my house but I could
never tie a proper knot
and I just stood there with
the rope around my neck
as the smell of smoked fish
covered me and I realized
that at night
I
am
broken
again.

Inspire the other

we left each other wondering
if there would ever be a tomorrow
and she told me that she loved
another man and I took it badly
and ended up unable to eat and drink
so I sat there and stared at the walls
and I wrote and I wrote bad poems
about the question of why did she
love another and how could she
love another.

as the pieces of me began
to come back together
I met a beauty from another
nation and she had a son and we
both devoured the other sensing
our losses and remembering our
past as we tore into love making
as if it would be the last time we
ever touched another human being
and in our wanton ways we were
able to put the last piece in place.

when I was on the road
I could search for women
who only wanted me
to take them and we would
play games and for awhile
I was rather good at taking them
to the place they needed to get to
and we would both dive into
the sorrow and the lust of one

another and I walked away
and out the door and down the road
I could hear her whisper to her
lover that there would never be
another to take his place.

centuries later I got a call
from her and she said she
missed me and said I was
always on her mind and I lied
and told her the same but I could
not tell her the truth that the
man she knew so long ago
died in a flame of destruction
and all that was left was the
need to inspire the other and she
hung up the phone and forgot all
about me and even though I had
glimpses of love I walked out
the door and down the road
as the day opened up
to the new love and passions
as the
song
bird
screamed.

I see the great cities

in the depth of the streets
there are creatures who
come out at night and they
seek to take the will away
from those dreads who sleep
on the ground with only
one blanket to cover
their lives.

the day begins and the
lovely people come out
of their mouse holes and they
seek that tasty piece of cheese
and they scurry from here to
there and they make small
weeping sounds as the city
overcomes them and they
race to get back to their
mouse holes and they dine
upon their rotten piece
of cheese.

the drunks open the bars
on the eastside of this
floating city with buildings
so tall they talk to God
on a daily basis and the drunks
sip cold watered-down beer and
the clinking of their glasses
creates a symphony of the
heavens and the gospel like
chorus of heroin addicts brings

the whole show to its
ultimate climax.

a child walks from corner
to corner asking if anyone
has seen her mother but the
people deny ever knowing her
and the child walks on into
the night and goes to every corner
of this city and moves on as
she and I go to the great cities
and we walk on searching for
our mothers who have been
missing for far too long
and now the missing fall
to the heavens of another
world
too far to see
too far to walk to
as the
rains
fall
yes
the
rains
fall.

I crawled the snaked path

into this moment I am
surrounded by all the snakes
of this earth and some of them
can talk and they tell me about
their lives and how their children
have slithered away into the
darkness and some tell about
the warmth of the sun and how
there was once a great snake
who could turn man into stone
and we had a good laugh
about that one.

as I pull the covers over
me the fan blows hot air
around my room and on the
floor there are hundreds
of films I have watched over
and over and I remember
even as a small child I would
hide away in old cinemas and
watch all the hits and I would
eat popcorn and watch the
snakes stick to the spilled pop
on the floor and the movie
would end and I would walk
out into the day and I would
become the movie and I would
become the hero as I walked to
my house and as I entered I would
slowly become alone.

once I crawled the snaked path
and it led me to the river and I
dove in and I swam down stream
and all the other snakes stood on
the shore and would cheer me on
as another big snake joined in
and we would race to the end of the
river and back again up to the
mountains and I was in the lead
when all of a sudden I could feel
the razor sharp teeth of the big
snake and poison entered me
and the movie ended and I floated
there unable to move as my feet
were stuck to the sticky floor
of this river and all the other snakes
wept as they knew my fate and as
the big snake who did not like to
lose opened its big mouth and I was
taken away down that snaked path
where all the heroes
walked out
into
the
day.

Crowded battle

say the words that
are hidden deep within
yourself and lean over and
kiss me on the lips and slip
your tongue and touch mine
and moan a little to remind me
that we belong together.

caress me with your golden
touch and walk away just a
little so I will follow you to
the end of it all and forgive me
for my transgressions as the sky
fills with stars and a moon so
white that all the dark of this time
shall be lit forever and walk away
a little more and turn and look
back so I know you are still
there for me.

lay down and accept me into
your body and wrap your arms
around me and hold me in
place and whisper in my ear
the words I love you and I will
stay here on top of you and
inside of you and as we slowly
move in and out the crowded
battle that has taken over our
moment rages on we will be hidden
from all the destruction that
mankind wages upon each

other for one book of God
versus the other and in time
we shall explode.

run away to the highest tree
and climb its branches and hide
in the forest of love and I will
search for you until I find you
covered in the moment
of us as the battle ends
and the sky
opens
its dream
of you
and I
and of you
my
love.

The magic of guilt

if ever you see me out
in an open space
sitting there having a
smoke and singing to the
winds with a bottle by
my side please just
keep on going your way.

if ever you find me on
the floor of a seedy
east end hotel please
call my mom and tell
her I have arrived
at the pearly gates
and I am ok as
Lucifer is right
behind me.

if ever I am kneeling
in a church please help
me pour the gasoline and
lock the one door and give
me some of that sacred wine
and together we can light
this bitch on fire and go
outside and await the sirens
and the screams and watch
this wooden church in our
ten thousand year old
village burn back
to the earth that was
stolen for his Holiness.

if ever I am fishing
and my boat goes down
and you see me in the water
please just leave me and
I will dive down into the
mystery of this mighty river
and I will become a water spirit
and if ever you need a favour
just tap your boat three times
and I will arrive and help
you through troubled waters.

if ever you see me
in love and holding hands
with my lover please
come and give us a hug
and tell us how special
we look and we will
thank you and then
we will
her and I
we will
walk towards
the sunset
as the
magic
of our
guilt
fades
to dust
and dust
and ashes
to ...

She stands

I begin my day the
same and when I get up
I light a smoke
and sip a hot coffee
and I look into the mirror
and I am no longer ashamed
at the scars on my face and it
is mostly around my eyes
where they had to stitch me
up after taking a few
kicks to the head with
the hardness of work boots.

the days are the same almost
repeated and the weather changes
as do the seasons and now today
the warm breeze of a warm
May day comforts me as
I sit at my desk and write poems
but even these poems are repeated
somewhere on an island
such as this one where
the birds come out singing
in the morning and by late
afternoon all is quiet.

bedtime is the same
as I take three pills as I have
for near eight years now
and I take one anti-depressant
and 2 anti-psychotic pills
that knock me out and flush

any dreams I may have had away
and I cannot recall the last dream
I could remember.

I think it was like this
as she stands above me
yelling at me to get up
and she points to the south
and I follow her and we are on
another island but it is
warmer and we are naked and the
world is no longer
around us and we walk the
beaches and I can still
feel the coolness of the sands
and we dive into the ocean
and she is gone as if she was
not even there and I awake
upon my bed alone and all
the sheets have fallen
and I am upon the island
of my bed as another
morning repeats
itself
into
madness.

Here we are

the moon was alone in a dusk
of blue and there were no clouds
to be found and the smell of baked
fish filled our home as it was
the first fish caught and the first
fish cooked slowly as the
rice pot brewed our rice
and we ate the fish and rice
and slowly we filled ourselves
with the gift from the river
as night came and the lone moon
shone upon us and we fell
asleep on a Sunday.

there were coyotes everywhere
and our dog barked and barked
at them and when a train's
whistle howled the coyotes
howled and howled to the moon
as it glowed white and all the fish
in the river swam upstream
as the river rose and rose up.

my arms and back ache from
a day of fishing and I go
out for a smoke and stare at
my old boat and I am amazed
that this old boat and my old
fishing net can still provide
supper for us and we are still
full from the night before as
morning brings the sunlight

and now every bird in the world
sings for us.

my passion to be with
another empties into the
fate that I am destined to be
alone and so I go out into
the sunny day and I am welcomed
by the song birds and the odd
call from a crow who sits on my
roof looking at me and it too stands
alone looking down on me and
together we accept our fate.

the soreness and ache of this
old man allows me to feel
a comfort in knowing that I am
the last of the river fishermen who
still can catch his supper and
provide for his children and the
sense of loneliness fades as I accept
the fact that I am a loner in a place
where the moon
shines in a sky of blue
as the coyote howls
the dog barks
and the angels
of this place
have come for me
on a blue sky moon

and
the
songs
of
tomorrow.

Beneath his breath

when I was younger I drank
and fought and drank and fought
and I was also the golden drug
addict and I would get my fix
every day as I would lie and
hustle all of mankind for a few
coins and the drip of my demon
would fill me up for hours as I
stared at the crumbling walls
and did not blink as the colours
of this century would go from
a tremendous red to a sour blue.

I used to live in the city and rode
a bike across the streets and the
masses would applaud for me
as I won every race that I entered
and I would jump the curb and travel
into the retched alleys and the demons
would come out and applaud for me
as I would hustle and lie for a
few coins to quench my empty heart.

in my twilight I am just a shell of a
man who won all the races
and the demons loved me
for who I was
as there was no hiding
from who I had become
and the city and the streets
told me to hate myself
but I never could

and I loved myself and the shell
of a man
who finally sat down
as the addicts came out
for that final race
and I placed second to Judas
who may have had more
coins
than
I.

Nothing at all

even in the hail of
bullets I find myself
watching another war and
I have seen a few in my
time and they all end the
same in a big fire ball
and all that is left are the
ashes of society and the
rules never change and the
world goes on as one man
hates one man.

the lost are never found
and they hide in the forest
among the spirits who
have come for a feast and
the fire burns cedar wood
and the smoke arouses all
the little ones who come out
of their holes and the feast
begins after the oldest spirit
of all says a small prayer of
thanks and the food is served
as the smell of cedar floats
across the sky and the little
ones giggle and laugh at the
tallest spirit there ever was
who tries to dance but
cannot find the beat of the song
and the little ones chew on deer
meat and giggle and giggle.

they built a church on our
island and told us to come
and pray and eat the body
of Christ and some did and
others stayed inside trapped
by the bottle in their hands
and the priest spoke about the
heavens above and how we
could all get there if we would
accept Christ and the words in a
big book and some did and others
went back home and opened a bottle
of cooking wine and the sour taste
was enough to open up the greatest
heaven that God could ever imagine.

they take their lives and I have seen
it before and I remember when my
grandfather stuck the gun in his
mouth and I remember another
friend who hanged himself because
he hated himself and so I wake up
every day and I am amazed at the
fact that I was given another day
to survive the past and live
the present to pray
if I did pray
I would pray
for
nothing
at
all.

Drank the wine

today a friend died
and all the people came
out and feasted and laughed
and cried a tear or two and the
drummers sang songs so old
that there were no words and it
was just grunts and whistles as the
sun came out and baked the earth
as the river flowed out to the ocean
where underneath the water
there was a dance held by
all the sea spirits and they
danced until the sun fell
off the edge.

a fat robin hopped around
and chewed on worms for
later on when it would come
back for the torn pieces and
stuff itself and fly away and
feed its young and the young
would scream in hunger
even if their bellies were full
and children are like that and they
cry and cry to be fed even if they
are full and so I go home and I bake
a fish and my young cry and laugh
at me and my old ways as the fish
bakes to perfection and I put a
piece of fish on a plate with a
couple of scoops of rice and my
children go to their corners of our

home and they still cry and laugh
at me as I sit and eat and dream
about a friend who on this day
passed on into the spirit world
where bake fish and rice
are on the menu.

if I fall please just leave me there
and move on to a better place
where all the fat birds rip apart
worms and the cries of the young
slowly fade into a very calm silence
and in that silence you will find me
as I drank the wine
ate the fish
cried a tear
swam with the ocean spirits
in a celebration
of life and death
and all the
wings of the birds
and their young
as the sun
bakes
us all.

Understanding

I heard that a sister
of mine from the
other side was beaten
by her lover at first I got
my gun and sat there in
my boat and I was going
to the mouth of the river
and I was going to put a
bullet in his head but the
night came and I had cooled off
so I decided I would use all
my secret hidden gifts and I would
put a spell on that man.

and they found him anchored
to the bottom of the sea and all
the fish he was to catch fed
upon him as he faded to the
skeleton he always was and the
drums pounded as they buried him
upon a hill overlooking the marshes
and as the dusk fell the earth
became a mosquito heaven.

my sister healed and we met
one evening at a big gathering and
she smiled to me and kissed me
on the cheek and she knew who
I was and what I could do and that
was all we ever said about that.

now I am in my boat
and thinking about going
up river to put a bullet in
another man who beat his lover
and the night came again and
I knew what I had to do so
I closed my eyes and sang
that sacred song as the mosquitoes
flew upriver to feed and feed upon
that evil man and all evil men
as we
sit here
understanding.

Leading the false

over time you come to
accept it all and you fall
asleep and you dream about
your boat sinking to the
bottom of the river and then
you wake up and you go to the
river and you get in your boat
and you throw your net
out and watch it drift and then
all of a sudden your net begins
to dance and you race over and
pick a twenty-five pound spring salmon
and throw it in your boat and begin
the day with a smile and a dream
of a sinking boat.

later when all the children have gone
to sleep you sit there on the floor
and you play cards and you cheat
to keep the game going as another
sleepless night is upon you and you
already know the dream so your
eyes dry up from not blinking and
you shuffle the deck and rig the
game as the slight sounds of
children sleeping pounds into
your mind and sleep never
comes as usual.

when the sunlight hits you
and the coffee is hot you
light a smoke and walk the

dog out into your finely cut
lawn and you watch the dog
chase rabbits but she never
catches one as they disappear
into the blackberries and you
inhale and exhale the crime
you never commit.

on the river and the sockeye
have arrived and you sweat
as the hot August sun burns
you a new disguise as you
throw the fish on ice and you
go back upriver and repeat
and put the net out and
sweat and throw the fish
unto ice and the sun burns
you as if this is your hell
this beauty of a tradition
that even over ten thousand
years has not changed and so you
go into that mind of yours
but all the dreams have faded
and you realize that you are
just a lone fisherman
playing a rigged game
and that
you
might
lose
this
one.

Hand in hand

this thought of never
finding love haunts me
to no end and I get up
every morning and I walk
out into the day and the
song birds sing a merry
tune as the dog runs around
looking for a good place to
pee and she does and I light
a smoke and breathe in the poison
and let it out into the coolness
of a June day.

when I walk to the forest
the eagles and the coyotes
follow me and then I see her
that crane
that ancient bird standing
still about to strike a fish
or a mole or whatever is
on the menu and she strikes
and I walk on into the forest
and all the spirits from the other
side come out and gather around
until we begin our ceremony
and we sing and dance around
a fire made by an old sasquatch
and the flames rise up to the sky
where all the owls have circled us
and they too dance this old dance.

when I sit down and write a poem
about her the ink flows so easily
and I remember her and how we
used to hide ourselves from
everyone and in this hidden
passion we were released and then
we would sit there and laugh about
this or that and then it was time
for me to leave and we never left
hand in hand no it was always my back
she saw as I walked home past the
celebration in the forest where I could
feel the flames of the fire
and as I entered my home
the owls would dive down
and take a rabbit each and they
flew away as the spirits
rejoiced and stayed up all night
as I went to sleep
and when I awoke
I was alone on my bed
as my lover
had vanished into
the flames
of a fire
made by
an
old
sasquatch.

In the other

the quietness of this place
has been here for centuries
and we accept this time and we
put one foot in front of the other
and we walk on to the next
ceremony and the fires are lit
and the plates of food are overflowing
and we devour our meal and sit
and laugh and cry about what has
happened in the past.

as we cleanup we are again
silent as we put our food away
and some we give to our dogs
as they have been here just as long
as we have and they protect us and
they let us know if there is trouble
coming either from up or down river
and when we are attacked by another
tribe our dogs are let loose and they
snarl and bite the invaders who have
come to take us away as slaves but
in most attacks we club
them to death and they
vanish back to where they
came from as our dogs bark.

when the colony came to
keep us from attacking
their queen they kicked
us out and we would watch
them from afar and we would

carry on with our lives and our
ceremonies as the fires are lit
tonight we dance and sing songs
so old that they scare the colony
and they sit there with their
weapons ready as if we are going
to attack them and we never
did no we sang and danced
for days as the colony wept
for their queen.

today the fort sits across
from my house and I can just
make out its walls and I go
about my life and try and teach
my children the ceremony and
so we light the fires and set
the table and we await our
visitors from up and down
river and they come and we
sing and dance until the
daylight arrives and we go
home as the fort sits empty
and forgotten as if frozen
in time as if it was never
there as we light the fires
of tomorrow
as the queen dies
and in the distance
a child raises her hands
as if thanking our people
for remembering

to feast and pray
as
we
appear
in
the
other.

Back home

on this island we live
and we die in grace and all
the people came for one more
meal and we share the fish
and the bread with you brother
so you will begin your new life
with a full belly.

they came and spoke great
words about you and how you
lived and how you were such a
great fisherman and all the women
sang a song for you and you carry
that song across the mountains
and you come to a place of rest
and all the animals wait for you
to speak to them and tell them
stories and the laughter of the
animals flows down into the
valley and back to our island.

they find fire cracked rock
as we build new houses for
our young and fire cracked rock
means our ancestors cooked
and feasted here thousands
of years ago and so do we
as the people gather to put
our brother away for his last
resting place across the river
on top of a hill surrounded
by eagles and hawks who

soar above and they call out
to you brother as the rocks
of this day crack in a hot fire.

the rains come but it is a
hot June day and all the family
sit quietly and mourn you brother
and then there is laughter as the
people remember all about you
and the life you lived as a
fisherman and you begin
your
journey
yes brother
go
back
home.

Heart stolen

when I was seven I fell in
love with a peach of a girl
who was much older than I and
she never knew I existed which
would be a pattern throughout
my days.

at fourteen there was a group
of us the same age and we
fooled around as best we could
but even then I could not understand
myself let alone another beauty
who I should have adored but
we were drunk and high on LSD
and it was our flower daze that
we all lived and we drank pure
whiskey and we smoked hashish
and dropped a hit of acid and then
we corrupted each other for twelve hours
as the rainbow of colours overcame
our being and we made love and we
made love as any fourteen
year old could ponder.

I used to get paid to fight
in bars and I met so many
young ladies and we courted
as if in the olden days and we
tormented the other and then
we moved from kingdom to
kingdom as if we were the
king and queen of an aged land.

now I listen to a soft ballad
over and over and I dream
about her that one that got
away from my sugar and was
the one who never could really
understand my gift of poetry
and I wrote and wrote only
for her but she left on a rainy
day like this one and my
heart was stolen for all to see
and they chanted
long
live
the
king.

Of the creation

went fishing and caught a
ten pound spring salmon and
I smiled as the seal popped his
head up and snorted at me and
then he swam away with his
belly growling and then I tried
to catch more but the river changed
and I snagged my net three times
and decided home was my best bet.

they say when you see a crane
on the shore fishing that you need
to be careful as they are an
ancient bird and they have seen
it all and they have been here long
before we ever took a fish and the
crane I saw today laughed as it
dove its beak into a small fish and
I smiled and my belly growled
and the seal popped his head
up and laughed at me.

people stare at me when I am
on the river fishing and I guess
we do look odd trying to catch
our supper when an extra large
pizza is just a phone call away and
when I go home it becomes a struggle
to pull my boat out of the water as the
river mud has been formed because
of the high water and my boat sticks
to the bottom as I pull my boat out and

my boots fill with water and later my
calves cramp up as I try and take my
boots off and try not to swallow too
many mosquitoes as my dog barks at
me as if laughing at my drama.

tomorrow we bury a friend of
mine and he would have laughed
about the seal as he had seen it all
on the river and he had fished almost
as long as the crane and the seal and
so I pay my respects to help the
family and I tried to catch more fish
for the family to feed their guests but the
river is like that of the creation
and we take what we can and move
on to another day on the river
with a full belly
a good mind
and the memory
of this man who
is on the other side
fishing and laughing
at us as we
failed
the
moment.

Blankets that are too small

heard a song about an old witch
and it made me think about
those who we do not see anymore
and they are the ones with powers
to eat fire and they do amazing
feats of strength and we used to
see them at our gatherings and I know
a few who are new to their gifts
and they are the ones we call healers.

in the dead of winter a fire glows
in the middle of the floor and all
have gathered to share stories and
some you have heard over and over
again and there is always a new one
spoken by the old ones who have
heard stories in their sleep and they
share them with us the young and we
remember them for a thousand years
and we repeat them at a thousand
gatherings and when the fire and the
flames attack the cold winds and we
laugh and we cry at the stories about
the great ones who could eat the flames.

when all have gone home I sit by the
fire and I can still hear the voices of the
dead and they tell me tales that never
made sense but today we are so in a rush
to forget that we never stop and listen
to the dead and their wonderful memories
of a world that was so simple and I try and

eat the flames but it just burns my tongue
and the dead laugh.

in the dead of winter the
winds pick up and blow it all
away and the trees bend and the
birds fly as high as they can and
dive down and land around me and they
hop around me as if in dance and I light
a fire and the birds vanish and I pull
a blanket that is too small over my head
and then the voices come and they
tell me about a great healer who could
turn people into stone and I look up
at a mountain and I think how great
that person must have been to be turned
into a mountain and as the cold winds
blow I hide beneath a blanket that is too
small to save me and all I hear are the
voices telling a story about a man turned
to stone and then I too
become
a
stone of a man
with
a
burnt
tongue.

Always her eyes

I used to believe that I could
stare at a woman in the eyes
and that I had the power to
make her love me and of course
I didn't and would feel rather
silly when she would look back
at me as if I was the Devil himself.

my first day of Catholic school
I got into a fight and the Sister
made us both punch the cement
walls as punishment and the
torture went on from then
and when I was seven a Priest
took me into a bathroom stall
and told me to touch him and to
pull down my pants and I thought
to myself that punching cement
was less tragic.

later when I was beautiful
young and old men would lure
me away from my home and they
tried to abuse me but as well
as being beautiful I was fast
and I could run and I did
I ran away from all the men
on earth and I ran and ran
until I too became a man
and that is when I decided
enough is enough and God
can go fuck himself and so

too the Devil and I sinned
with all the girls I could
and I again became
beautiful.

in my fifties now I sit and
wait for her to appear but she
never does appear so pure
that I know she is the one
for me so I wait and light a
smoke and put it out
and light another and I sit
here so beautiful awaiting
her to enter and all of a sudden
there she is and it is always her
eyes that punish me for all I have
done and for all that was done
to me and I realize in my world
there is no God and there is no
evil no just me
this broken
unloved man
who thinks he can stare
into your eyes
and
make
you
love
him.

Fascination for me

a boat ride brings me around
the corner of our island and it
is a calm day on the river and
there are only a few boats and
we all want to catch a fish and
tell tall stories of how we did
so I throw my net into the
river and drift down past our
island and there is only silence
as I watch the corks on top of
my net and I await the quick
dance that will tell me that a
fish is in the net and it does
not come as I drift past our
island and I begin to pull in my
net and all around me the trees
on the shoreline sway to the
rhythm of an old song and
I pull my net out and turn my
boat back up river to do it
all again.

this morning I began to
remember my days in high school
and how death would have been
easier but I tried to fit in but I was
a bum
a con
a liar
so I stood in the shadows
and sold drugs and I smoked
drugs and I drank pure

lemon gin and puked it all
over and I reminded myself
that this is who I was and I would
fight anyone and at any time just
to feel the pain of it all and some
I won and most I lost and my face
today shows the scars of one too
many beatings and I ended up
dropping out of school and working
boring jobs and hustling the streets
and still I drank and I would black
out and wake up in jail not
remembering the night before so
I kept going until one day I said
fuck it and quit it all and then the
real me appeared.

I am so they say a manic depressive
but my outlet was anger and fighting
still is a part of me as I await the next
round and I do not drink or do drugs
but I am quite insane but I am not
to be feared as the only harm that
will come will be to myself so we all
await my final performance and how will
I go and we wonder if it will be like
my Grandfather with a gun in his
mouth or will it be like all those who
tied the rope to a tree or will I one
day take my boat and instead of my net
I will throw myself into the water
and the fish will have a fascination for me

as I fall to the bottom not so much
the hero or the villain but someone
who could not become
no
he
could
not
become.

Take this hurt

a photograph of a group
of Indians praying on a hill and
in the background a Father in black
robes is the only one that is smiling
and after the picture the tired souls
get in their canoes and paddle
upriver to their village and go about
their day as the rains fall and the
Father goes to his small wooden
church and he disrobes and stands
in the rain naked and he looks to
the sky for a sign from God but it
never comes even years later when a
young Indian man cut the throat of
this Father and the Indian man
whispers into the Father's ear
as he bleeds out: take this hurt.

in an alley the needles poke
the poor addicts like a giant
voodoo doll and the pain is felt
every time the heroin flows
and one girl she is from across
the water from an island where
the Indians are older than time
and she walks as best she can trying
to keep her wiggle in time with
her addiction and an old dirty
man asks her to service him
and she does and walks away
with a ten dollar bill and goes
to the dealer who gives her what
she really needs and she squats

in the piss and shit as the rains
fall and she jams that needle into
her neck and she floats away as
her mouth opens and she says:
take this hurt.

on a reserve not this one but
one up river a bit a young
man sits on the edge of a
mountain and he sips his
cheap wine and he talks
to himself as his mind is nothing
but mush and he teeters on
the edge of a cliff daring himself
to fall and he does he falls and
glides a bit but in the end he
comes smashing down to the
earth and his arms are spread out
like he was trying to catch hold
before he died but he did and all
the mountains of the earth stood
up and looked down on another
poor man and his cheap bottle
of wine who died and on the way down
he screamed: take this hurt
and the words echoed
for over a century
of the next despair
that
you or I
would
imagine.

Beauty of our people

we came from the sky
it is said we were at first
wolves and we could run
and never get tired and so
we became human beings
and we were told by a great
spirit that we were to take fish
from the river and to always
give something back and so we
did and we are still here in the
same village that has been lived
in for ten thousand years and our
children look at us and wonder
how we kept going after all that
has happened but we do
everything with a good mind
and from birth to the end we
care for all of our people and we
never get tired.

in the distance a train blows
its horn and the song birds
are all out and some bathe
in mud puddles and others
chase one another from tree
to tree and then one rain drop
falls from the top of a tree and hits
every leaf on the way down and as
it falls from the last leaf it comes
to rest on the head of a song bird
who bathes in a puddle of mud and the
train disappears into the valley as our

people awaken for the day and they
rise up and gather by a fire made by
a healer and we burn plates of food
for all those we have lost and they come
to the smoke and they eat their favorite
plates of food and the people watch as
the fish and the rice are caught by the flames
and the smoke feeds the forgotten as another
train comes around the corner unaware
of the sacred fire and the hunger of the
lost.

at night an owl hunts for mice and river
rats and the owl is silent as it glides
across our island and then it sees a
rabbit and dives down and clutches the
rabbit in its claws and the moon shows
itself and the owl feasts and we know who the
owl is as it is one of us and we know this owl
to be as old as time and we know this owl
as it is the beauty of our people
transformed
but
never
forgotten.

The truth

the birth of a child is what
this village needs as we bury another
elder and we need more laughter as
the June rains are falling and the wind
sits quietly in the back waiting for the
clouds to fade away and a blue sky
comes out of somewhere and we place
the last shovel of dirt on our elder
and we wait for the young mothers to
have their spring babies and we wait.

there once was a medicine woman
who could control the time and she
held it to slow us down and if we
needed something done right away
she would blow ashes from the fire at us
as we slept and when we awoke
we got to it and we harvested the
summer fish and we harvested the
fall fish for our smokehouses and we
salted the fish and hung it up and we lit
the fire and she would slow down the
burning wood and the sweet smoke
rose up as the hanging salted fish
became our future.

in the depth of a cedar forest
there was word of another man
who could control the weather
and he froze the ground and he
froze the river and our people
ate salted fish and tried to keep

warm but this man made it so cold
that our people froze where they
stood and we could not bury them
until the man in the cedar forest
decided enough was enough
and we had suffered for
a long time so he blew
ashes at us as when we were
all asleep and in the morning
when we awoke the sun had
burned all the frozen ground
and the river began to move
again and we went out and we
took ten sturgeons from the bottom
of the river and this is the truth
and I know this because today
I got into my boat and time stands
still as the man in the cedar forest
blows ashes that
become
rain.

His new honours

I have spent some time in a
few madhouses and not that I was
forced to
it was I did not want to
live anymore and I had stopped
eating and so I walked into the
stream of craziness and accepted
that I did belong there and those
I met along the way accepted me
as well and we had a good time
of it.

in the morning I would awake to
the sound of a whistle as the guy
in the next room was of course a
lifeguard and he was supposedly
a very good swimmer in his younger
days and now he can be found on
the third floor section fifteen of this
place and he whistles to those who
are breaking the rules of this pool
which of course is an oddly painted
hallway consisting of drab lighting
and the smells of men who do not
care for themselves and the
whistle gets me up and I dress
and look at my face in the mirror
and today I almost recognize who
I used to be.

in the evening after a meal of
tea and toast and that's a start for me
because I have only been here for a

few days and already I want out
and after my cold tea I walk back to
my room and I am greeted by Christ
who says welcome my child to me
and I say hello and he kneels in the
corner and recites a recipe for some
meal he must have had when he was
a child and I lay on my bed and I close
my eyes and when I open them Jesus
is standing over me chewing on an
apple and I thought to myself how
interesting that Jesus is eating the
apple and as he chewed I swear
I saw a snake come out of one of
his eyes and I screamed and Jesus
screamed and the lifeguard whistled
as someone had pissed in the pool
and all I could think of was how
many steps it was to the front door
of this place and how I would
just leave and go back
to this
crazy world
we
all
live
in.

To make this

we loved each other and we were
forbidden by all those people who
decided it was enough but
we loved and we made love
in the darkness of this mystery
of who we had turned into and
I was the greatest lover of the time
and she was the beauty that all
beauty started from and we made
love in the darkness of our secret
and we fooled only ourselves and
we kept going until the world erupted
into war and all the earth was destroyed
by that one bomb we all forgot about
and she died in my arms and I took
her last breath and I stood up and
walked in to the hell fire of this earth
and as I did the earth spun and spun.

in another life I met her by a tree
and we made love standing up and
she screamed for mercy but all I could
do was stay inside her and she kept me
there for a century and we made love
by that tree as the world became covered
in ice and all life was turned to ice and we
stayed connected until the warm winds
picked up and melted us and we became
the river and we flowed forever embraced
in a lover's dance that went on and on.

on a street on the east side of creation
I kiss her on the lips and we trade tongues
and we invade the streets as we have a taste
of the glaring pipe and we dance an addict's
dance of destruction and we walk out into
the world that is both fire and ice and we
make love in an alley as the people who
corrupted us walk on by and never give
us a second glance and we make love
in a final moment as the fire of the pipe
destroys our minds and we stare at each
other and we know we have seen this life
before in another life
in another time
when the earth
was both a fire
and it was a cold
place
where
lovers
die.

There was more

when we fall from grace we
fall and fall and then we get
up and we go to the mountain
and bathe in the snow fed pools
until the stink of yesterday peels
off and we are re-born.

we run up to the tallest peak
and our sweat attracts the bugs
and they dine upon our blood
but we keep running and running
until we come to the top and we
look down upon our past and ask
forgiveness for all our sins but we
never get too clean as we have
to have some deception in our
lives and so we go home and smile
and those around us smile back
and they do not know how much
we have been forgiven for.

at an old reservation church
our people gather and kneel
and they recite the text of God
and sing a few hymns about a saint
or two who sacrificed themselves
for God or the story goes and the
church empties as the Indians go
home to their squalor and open
a bottle or two and they drown
in the self-pity that comes
with believing in a God who

died for our sins or so it goes
and the drunks look out into
the night as every star in the
sky glimmers as if God himself
created them.

there were more moments
to share as we sit here in this
life and we are chosen by God
to fulfill his thoughts but sometimes
they do not fit us as we believe in
something older than any God
and we do not read from a book
as our words are repeated over
and over and we sing songs given
to us by the winds and the sounds
of the forest and so we bathe
and we run and we sweat and there
was more hurt but some of us
are lost and we sip the poison
of man
and the taste
resembles God
if
he
only
knew.

The fact is

empty streets are washed by
west coast rains and then the
dreads come out of their holes
and begin the migration to the
corners where all the treats are kept
and they swim in the rivers created
by the rains and they perform so
eloquently and the pace they keep
is only heightened by the drugs they
are on and they dance in the waters
as the sun comes out of another
corner and the dreads swim back
to their holes as the rains dry up.

working girls come out in all
shapes and sizes and outfits of the
day and they sell their lives to the
highest and the lowest bidders and
those monsters are always there
and they are men who would eat
their own hearts if it excited
them into the frenzy they need
to get off in this street where
women are taken and taken
and they fade away as their pretty
dresses fall to the ground and they
are picked up by another and she too
fades as the monsters attack her and
take her to another place over there
past all the horrors of mankind.

children play in the shit of yesterday
and they laugh and throw their minds
into the mix and they too fade away
as the monsters come for them and these
men would eat their own hearts as they
take another child and they bury them
over there where east meets west and
the rains fall one more time and wash
away the dreads of this street
and the sun falls back into a hole
as the night becomes a new world
and it is one that moves a bit slower
as
the
monsters
come
for
me.

Going to go to sleep

this pen is running out of
ink and I should stop writing
poems that seem to be about
the same thing over and over
but I cannot and it's like a demon
in my mind and the words flow and the
images are painted and if I could I would
just lay down here and never write again
but we all know the answer to that one
as I pump out the blood ink and turn
it into paradise.

we met her and I at a gathering and we
knew each other well and one day she
called me and told me how she felt
and I drove to her and we fucked in
my truck and it was a cold January night
and we fucked and after we both had
a cigarette and then I dropped her off
near her house and she smiled to me
that wicked smile that lovers have for
each other and we both met a few times
after that cold night and she is in my
dreams now and she is in a poem and
sometimes she appears in many of my
poems and only she knows who she is
and as I close my eyes I remember her
wicked smile.

there are those out there who think
they can judge me and my hat off to
them as they were close but how could

anyone know of the demons inside of me
and the things I have done in my past
that only I know about but they judge and
I hold in my secrets as they are all I have
left for the grave and when they bury me
I am going to sleep and all the wicked
smiles of my life will warm me
in
the
coldness
of
the
earth.

Cut away

in the darkest times I find
myself alone on my boat
and my net is out and we drift
past an eagle's nest and a small
deer comes out of the trees for
a cool drink of water and then
my net begins to dance and I race
over and pull up my net and there
is the best of this time a twenty pound
spring salmon that will feed my family
for days.

as I cut away the memories that will
haunt me till the day I go to the other
side I am left with the glory of the gift
of my children who have grown into
wonderful spirits and it is they who
keep me going as I mend the holes and
rips in my old fishing net and the
mosquitoes eat me alive and a soft rain
falls and I am almost done mending my
net as the rain falls harder as I finish and
jump off my boat and check everything
else needed tomorrow for six hours
of fishing given to us by some queen
from across the ocean and I make sure
I have enough gas and my truck is ready
to drop my boat into the river and then
I go inside and see my son and I am
reminded of my glory.

again on the river and there are more
big boats and that means more nets in
the water and I throw my net out and
drift down past the eagle's nest
and there are no deer today and the
rains hold and the mosquitoes have
vanished and then my net dances
in the middle and I race over and
I think to myself that this is my
glory and there is nothing left
to
cut
away.

Through the kiss

I have tried the real world
and all my failures have taught
me to find a room like this one
and to stay here because out there
I am there for all to see and I am
there for all to rip apart and when I
go outside I have to remember the right
words to speak as what I really want to
say is: fuck off and leave me alone with
your pettiness and your wonderment
about life and so I stay in this room
with my thoughts.

I have tried to be famous but
I could not fit into the clothes that
you have to wear when you parade
yourself around in hope that all the
people will see the shine of my
smile and again I have forgotten
the words so I take a bow and say:
fuck you all and your pettiness and your
self-pity and get on with it as this is
all we get and you all waste it as I try
and pull up my pants that were made
too big for me.

it is through the kiss that I am saved
and when we first met and when we
first made love at your place we were
like animals and I felt you made
me belong and I knew all the words
but when you deceived me all I could

do was yell: fuck off and leave me alone
and it was through the kiss that I will
always remember you as I sit in my room
with a candle burning and I sit here in
my self-pity as the flame of the candle
flickers
so
perfect.

For the evening

we welcome those who have lived
before us and we feed them as we
throw them a few blankets to keep
them warm as the snow falls across
from us as we sit in the hot sun of the
end of another month of June.

this is our time to live and to regret
and to live and to pray that our children
will not suffer as our older ones did when
they were sent away on a train to a far
away island and they were taught to fear
the Lord and they still do some of them
and some of them stay inside when the sun
is out and they pray for the evening to not
hold any thoughts of so long ago when
they were five or six and they were
homesick and the servants of God told
them that in order to get to heaven
they would have to kneel and some even
after fifty years later some of our older ones
still kneel inside their homes as they are
ashamed to come outside and accept our
ways that were here long before any God
laid claim to us.

a child throws cedar into the river and
it floats down past a great city and out
to the ocean and it keeps going
until a child grows into a human being
of a lost tribe of people who have lived
here for centuries and the child does

not kneel no the child raises his hands
up to the spirits who have come over
and they are cold and hungry and we
feed them.

when night comes again we all dress
for the evening gathering and the drums
begin and the people rejoice in their
sorrow as some of us never came back
after being sent away to learn about
God and his house of hell and they are
still those who did come back and they
are ashamed as they look out their
windows as the young gather and drum
and sing and pray to old spirits that have
come back for a taste of fish
a warm blanket
the memory
of our
people again
lifts us up
to the sky
as God
steps aside
as he
knows not
what
he
has
done.

Eyes for weeping

all around me the spirits
sing and dance and they tell me
to get on with living and I do
as I put my boat in the water and
go around our island to the main
channel and I throw my net
out and light a cigarette as an
eagle glides by me and screams
as the silence of the day is broken.

nothing in my net the first time
down river and nothing in my net
the second time so the third time
I throw my net closer to the shore
and sure enough a fish hits and I race
over and pull it up but it is so heavy
and I struggle to get it into my boat
but I do and she is a beauty of
twenty-seven pounds and you can do
nothing but smile as the eagle screams.

that day I was to catch four more
spring salmon and all was going well
and it was time to go home so I headed
in and the day was again quiet as the
eagle was now dancing and singing
with all the spirits and I kept smiling
and lit another cigarette and pushed my
boat back up river to our village
and I thought to myself that these
eyes were for weeping so I began to
cry and remember all the people

we had lost and how quieter the river
had become without them fishing
beside me and as my boat came to our
village I let out a scream so loud it
shook the trees and the eagle turned
his head
and
he
smiled.

Black wings

at the moment I find that
all is good and we are carrying
on just fine as a moon so bright
it lights the world and I find
that this could be the perfect
time to be alive and it is for
me and my children who sleep
as I awake and go outside for a
smoke and our dog follows me
and she runs around barking
at rabbits and I finish my smoke
and we go back into our house
and is quiet as the fire moon burns.

the black wings of a hundred birds
shade the morning and the sky
becomes a shadow but even this
is a good time to be alive and so I turn
and enter the day and it is like yesterday
as there is nobody for me to talk to and the
kids lay in their beds and I begin my day
alone as usual and it is like this almost
every day for me and it is not that I pity
myself it is the way it is as black wings
cover the sky and I sit alone in my room
and I write poems and this is where all
my friends are and they come to me upon
the page and we laugh together as I cry
a few tears not in sadness but in the joy
of knowing such wonderful people.

the song changes on the radio and it
is a soft ballad about lost love and I sit
alone in my room again and no one
spoke to me today but I carried on and
I fed the kids and I fed the dog and I
smoked about twenty cigarettes and
as I tossed each one away they became
an inferno of who I used to be.

another night comes and the moon
is nothing but a sliver and the clouds
are coming over the mountains and the
rains begin to fall like the tears of those
who used to talk to me but
again I become alone in a room
where the black wings
of who I am
open up in unison and they
cover all of
me
again.

Reflected light

all the women who have loved me
throw coins at me as I dance down
the dirt and smells of a city street
and all my friends stand on the edge
of a building and they look down upon
me as I twirl in a perfect circle and I shuffle
on down the shit of this street as all the
women who loved me come up to me
and they kiss me on the mouth and some
slip a tongue in and they taste the booze
from the night before but they do not
taste the heroin that I jammed into my
arm an hour ago and all my friends applaud
for me as I twirl once more and then I fall
down in the street as the women who loved me
cry.

being who I am and what I look like now
is quite frightening as my past has been
quite normal and I find this city to be just
fine for me as I beg and steal enough for
a hit and a cigarette and I find the needle in the
pile of a dead man and I swim away as the
heartbeat of this glorious day carries me
to my home and there I see my children
and they do not see me as I float all around
our reservation and I float back to the city
and I am a pile of shit and clothes and I open
one eye as all the girls come around me and kick
me to see if I am breathing and I do
I breathe.

my girl and I hold on tight
as we smoke some cool ice and
the heat of the pipe is enough to
warm us and the reflected light
of these two humans shines the
alley way as the perverts come out
to play and all the beggars go home for
a piece of cheese and me and my girl
and the shine of the reflected light
burn and burn as the pipe narrowly
condemns me to stay here
in this alley
this time
this putrid existence
of two addicts
in love
one
more
time.

Own teachings

if the rains come I will
start a fire and watch the
smoke rise and go into the sky
and all the birds will squawk at me
and I will smile and hope them well
as I go to my boat and go out into
the river and throw my net out and
light a smoke and watch the sky fill
with noisy birds who do not even like
me as a fisherman.

the day brought no fish and it is
like that on days when the sky is
black and the smoke rises and makes
all the birds disappear as a seal pops
his head up at the end of my net and we
share a smile as we both know there are no
fish today so we both go home and hide under
the blanket.

our own teachings are very old
and very simple and we were told
by our elders as they were told by
their elders and so on and on and one
teaching I like is to always do things
with a good heart and a good mind
and all will go well and so I do I
listen to all the words shared at any big
or small gathering and so in this life I follow
the teachings as I light another fire and
the noisy birds have all gone to sleep and

the silence is what I need and I open my
ears and I listen to the old stories that I have
heard for a lifetime.

in the end we all have days when your
net is empty and you sit by a warm fire
as the seal and the noisy birds gather
upon a mountain and they begin to yell
at me and I tell them to be quiet as an
old man from upriver is telling a tale
about a great Sasquatch and I tell the seal
and the birds to stop yelling because I have
never heard this story and that old man
finishes and we thank him with a few dollars
and I smile as I look into the fire and all I see
is a great Sasquatch walking up a mountain
and scolding the seal and all the birds as they
become quiet with
their
own
teachings.

Laid her head down

on a corner a girl stands
and she is singing a song from
where she came from which was
a small reservation upriver not quite
to the mountains and the song she is
singing is heard by all women of the streets
and they too begin to sing and the city becomes
a song from somewhere upriver
and all the people stop for a moment
and they listen to the song and all the
women of the world for a moment
are saved.

the girl who sang that song walks
across the street and she digs in her
pockets for some change and she buys
some cigarettes and lights one as an old
drunk man comes up to her and begs for
a smoke and she gives him one and as she
hands it to him she touches his hand and
she remembers who he once was and she
smiles and the old man thanks her and he
turns to walk away as the girl says:
goodbye, Father.

as night comes so do all the animals of the
city and they prey upon the women who
sang a song from upriver somewhere and
the animals take away some of the women
and they no longer sing and the girl who sang
the song and shared a cigarette walks on home
to her village as she has had enough of the pain

and she walks into her village as all her people
come and greet her and hug her and tell her
she is welcome home and the girl goes to her
Father's old home and there is no one there
and she goes inside and she sits down and she
begins to sing her song and all the women of
the world are saved as this home
this village
is where she
laid her head down.

Meeting ground

with the depths of who
I am appear and fade
I am still just a man
of a few words and I listen
to all who come near enough
for me to hear and I listen
to their stories of how they have
lived their life and how life
has forsaken them.

when it is just me I go inside
my mind and I go outside and
I stand still as a cool wind
blows and I close my eyes
and I relive all the good memories
of this retched life and for me this
is a good meeting ground and as
I stand still the earth rotates and
I begin to rise above the ground
and I open my eyes and I can see
my village and everyone is asleep
as I rise up and relive my life
over and over and I love it this
feeling that I am a good man
a good father
a good lover
and then I come down to earth
and my feet touch the ground
and I close my eyes and this
is peace on earth I think to
myself as the winds go away
and the rains begin to fall.

my fingers are all cut and to me
it always means there are spirits
around and as I bleed I smile and
laugh at the spirits and their little
tricks to torment me and to cause me
to fail and I just fail and bleed
and smile as I know this will stop
when I have given enough of my body
to the spirits so I go and stand in that
same spot and I close my eyes as the
world and all its passion flow through me
as an old lover of mine walks up to me
and kisses me as the world
spins
one
more
time.

Followed by

the river flows right
outside of my home and
I have lived here for ten
thousand years and today
I am a lone fisherman raising
three kids on my own and we
have a dog who chases and eats
rabbits and we used to have cats
but the coyotes ate them all and now
the dog rules the home and she now
sleeps on my bed where there should
be a woman but they too all left long
ago and in this life I am quite happy as the
dog barks.

I went fishing the other day and I
fished hard for six hours and came
home with nothing and I tried yes
I tried and tried and I threw that net
everywhere on the river and not even
a nibble and I went home happy as this
is who I am and sometimes the river says
fuck you, fisherman there are no fish
for you and so I go to bed and close my eyes
as the dog barks.

in the morning I awake
before the sun comes up and
I let the dog out and she
chases rabbits and she stops
and scratches as I light
a smoke and inhale deep

to feel the burn of nicotine
and exhale the smoke out
into the morning
as the sun comes up
from the east of this
village where we have
all lived since we fell
from the sky and I finish
my smoke and go inside
and stare at the pile of dirty
dishes and the dog barks to be
let in and I do I let her in and she
stares at me to feed her and I do
I give her some dry food as the sun
rises on another day
of
my
eternal
self.

And the Indian

we all have a spirit and we do not
get to choose them as they choose us
when we are reborn into this time and
we meet them in all different places
and I met mine at an old gathering in a very
small and smoky home and all the old people
had come to meet me and to welcome me
to their world and they told me to sit down
and cry and so I did I cried and cried the
night away and my old spirit sat beside me
and smoked the cigarettes I had brought for him
and when the sun came up he gave me a hug
and said he would see me around and I walked
out into the day and lit a smoke and I walked
across the mountains and a river and an ocean
and a forest and when I arrived I sat down and
cried.

there are all kinds of spirits and it is up to us
on how we see them and in most cases we are
loved by them we have known them long before
they became spirits and some are family and others
are the lost and forgotten of this
world and they have no one here and
they have no one there so they look around
for those of us that are living and if we have
no one those spirits join us and they help us
and they also play games and if you hear
strange noises in the night or if you drop
a piece of food you know they are around
and they are laughing at us as we drop
a sandwich upon the floor.

I am protected by the spirits who have
chosen me and I have to take care of
them and I do this by burning plates
of food for them and I raise my hands up
to them when I catch a fish in my net and
I smile when they take things from me
like a sock or a book I was reading and I
swear I put it down somewhere in my
house but it is gone and you can hear the
pages turning in the middle of the night
when we are asleep.

I believe I should be ok in this life
because I have lived before as I believe
we all have and I am not anything great
but I am a fighter and I fought all the way
through this life and as I go into becoming
a simple man I am protected by an old
spirit who shares a smoke with me from
time to time and we share a laugh
as the pages of my lost book
turn.

With his new honours

I closed my eyes and I could
finally see all of my friends and
my family and it was a good dream
and I have kept it hidden inside of me
as the real me
rages.

I want to speak out and tell the
people that they should be grateful
for all that has been given to them
but some of them just keep on
using our people for themselves
and in the end they
rage.

our children watch our every
move and it is so easy for them to
take a sip of booze and smoke something
and these days you never know what the
poison is and our children
rage.

when a child is born I give them
an Indian name that they will carry
for the rest of their lives and they
must protect that name and not
dirty it in any way and they must
look to the elders for guidance and some
do and some do not as the elders
rage.

with his new honours one of our
young jumps into the river and he is
gone before we could even scream
and we never find him and he now
has become a spirit of the water and he
swims deep down and discovers who he
could have been as the river
rages.

I again close my eyes and I see how
fucked up I really am and even the
medication does not help and so I write
poems like this one and I beg for mercy
as the voices in my head
rage.

Today in the growing sunlight

on the streets again and all is
going to shit and I try to get back
to where I came from but the
seasons are all screwed up and the
sun is out and then the sun is not
and the rains prepare themselves
and they do not fall and the winds
pick up and then they are gone across
the ocean and I am still here staring
at my shoes telling my body to move
but the drugs tell me to stay one more
time, please.

when I was young I was so handsome
and all the girls wanted me inside them
and I obliged them and you know who
you are and I know who I was but now
my tangled face and my sunken eyes
look through the morning mist of a
city's beginning and my shoes move one
step forward and I steal enough for another
whisper of the demon who controls me and
I get it from the corner over there just past
the pigeons and I squat in a corner and I begin
my existence away into the morning mist.

I once ran into a girl who told me
that I was her everything and we would
dance down the alley and all the ghosts
would come and we would hold a
poor man's ball and all the men with
guitars would play for us a poor man's

waltz and we were so perfect as our shoes
did what they were told to do and we
finished our dance as today in the growing
sunlight her and I escaped our tragedy and
destroyed the demon if only to begin again
as she fell and went home and I tried to
follow but these damn shoes
these
damn
shoes.

Words very easy

they grab a hold of you when
you are doing something so simple
and you drop so low that even
getting from under the blankets is
like lifting rocks off of your body
and when you do get up your mind
is still lying there comfortable
upon your pillow and you venture
out to your day and you cope with it
as you drop some bread into the
toaster and you sip your hot coffee
and you light a smoke and you look
behind you but there is no one there.

in the evening you do the same routine
and they say to repeat is insane and you are
you are insane but in a good way and you are
able to hide enough of it so your kids do not
realize the changes and you dive into your
bed and you let the medication take hold of
you as the voices tell you enough is enough.

once a voice told me that no one liked me
and everyone was laughing at me and my mild
ways and I saw them laughing at me and I just
would smile knowing that they knew nothing
at all about me because if I had been asked
about me I would not have an answer for them
so they laugh and I smile and later when I dive
upon my bed I cry the good cry as the blanket
shrouds my fears.

one day I will be able to speak about what
was done to me and how I have left it hidden
for so long but for now I hide it deep within
myself and the voices tell me to go outside
and walk to the river and jump in but I never
do as the words were very easy
and the voices take turns laughing
at me as I crawl beneath the blankets
and
smile.

Every once in awhile

upriver from here I have
brothers who have the gift of
singing and drumming songs that
are so old they sound so wonderful
and these men are at all the gatherings
and they lift up everyone if they are down
and the songs are so simple that you
can join in and sing your heart away.

in the city there are no songs
just misery and despair and the lost
Indians gather and they remember a man
who passed away while he sipped his
last drink and his friends come together
and they left a few words as there was
drinking to be done and they all faded away
into the hell of a city that prides itself
on its look.

when one world meets the other
you know where you are from
and some try to get back and others
could care less about their home as
that is where the abuse was and so
they linger in the city for too long
and the streets eat them up in one
swallow as the glass pipe is burning
one more time and when they leave
this world their ragged friends gather
and there are no songs for them as
in this world there are no men or
drummers to carry a tune.

we could sit here and pity them
but who has time for that
so we sit in our villages along
the river and we can only pray
for those who are lost and for the
women who have vanished from
us all and so we stand on the
shores of the river and we drum
one more song as every once in
awhile our worlds join as one
and the Indians dying in the
beautiful city hear us
as if they
had
all
along.

Sense the distance

over time you begin to understand
who you are and why you are here
and that is ok and you keep that to
yourself and let others walk their walk
but you have to try and keep it together
for your kids and you do as you rise up
each day and walk out to the morning
as the July rains fall and the day begins
as the sense of distance of you and
reality is actually quite close.

in my yard I have racked my fishing nets
for the fish that are coming up river and I
check my nets and mend any breaks and rips
and the dog stares at me and wonders when
it is time to eat and I sit down to mend a hole
created by a seal and the twine and needle
and my eyes do the work and the hole is
mended as best I could and I begin to bag up
the net and then I begin on my second net
as you always should have a second net
as the river sometimes can destroy a net
if you throw it in the wrong places and as I
mend my second net the dog stares.

for me the sense of distance
comes in all sorts of colours and
meanings but I am ok as I slept
through the night as the hot July
rains fell and wetted all that needed
to be wetted and today like every day
I light a smoke and I breathe in deep

and I feel calm and sorrowful as all the
hate I have seen in my life decides to
cloud my mind but I move on and put
my shoes on as the sense of distance
from dying is much further away as I
walk out into the July rains and all the
spirits gather to see if I am ready
and I tell them no not today
as the fish are here
and
the
dog
hungers.

What appears

I pull off a hangnail and wince
in pain and we all have moments
of torture to ourselves so we pull
and pull off pieces of our body and
toss them to the side and we have
a perfect body as parts of us bleed a
little and when I am done pruning my
being I get up and dress in the same
clothes I wore yesterday and I slip
on an old pair of sneakers I have
worn without socks for over a year
now and I pull a t-shirt on and put on
a baseball hat I will wear until the dog
gets a hold of it and chews it to shit and
then I stare at myself in the mirror as a
drop of blood falls from my fingers as
I purify and go and face the world.

I get a coffee and burn a smoke
and I go to my office and I sit
down and turn on some music
and I open my book and pick up
my pen and I turn nothing into
nothing as the tune on the radio
blares and the poems fall so
brilliantly and I create nothing to
nothing and this is who I am a very
lost poet and fisherman and father
and a man once loved by the millions
but now I wear the same clothes and
the same shoes of yesterday and this is
what appears to you if you ever see me
on the outside of my being.

parts of me have fallen off
and I work with what is left
and there in the corner is my mind
where words spin and spin and I grab
a word and place it upon the page
and from there I join the words
as a poem arises to look back at me
and sees that I have a new hat and I
have new shoes and I look good
as I am
so it seems
I
am
what
appears.

They can howl

I sit and play cards with a
sasquatch I met when I went to
bathe in the mountain fed waters
near a village where all the healers
live and I dealt out five cards each
and the sasquatch smiled and said he
was good and I tossed down two cards
and took two more and I had a straight
but it was nothing compared to his
four aces and he smiled and took
my money and began to walk away
leaving his footsteps for the people
to find later and he turned and smiled
and I knew he had cheated and I smiled
too.

I met a coyote by a fire and she
came close to me and snuggled
up to me as she was cold and wet
from the west coast showers and she
said she was hungry so I gave her some
of my fish and she snuggled closer and our
eyes met and we both fell asleep by the
fire and in the morning when I awoke
she was gone as was all my fish and in
the distance I could hear her children
howling as the coyote fed them my fish
and I smiled as I snuggled with my empty
belly growling.

on the river I caught a fish who could
speak my old language and he said that
he knew all the healers and that he was

given life forever as long as he returned
home every four years and we talked a
bit more as I knew a few words of my
language and I let him go and he began
to swim upriver on his way home and we
met again later when I was at the end
of my life and we talked some more and
he said the healers upriver were waiting for me
and I smiled as I let him go and he turned
and said he had met the sasquatch and he too
had been cheated and he said he had met
the coyote and her children and that they
had tried to eat him but that he had swam
away as they
howled
and
howled.

A strange confession

I know this young lady who has
lived more than most and she
carries so much sorrow that she
smiles whenever we meet and
yesterday she looked at me and asked
why I was so sad and I did not have an
answer so I said a bunch of things that
would make it alright to be sad but really
I wanted to tell her that this is how I always
look and sadness is just a part of my
clothing and she smiled and we hugged
and we said goodbye until the next time
and she vanished as all her sorrow stayed
with me and became a new piece of
clothing for me.

yesterday evening I was driving
back from the delta and I had a
massive anxiety attack and coughed
up phlegm and spat it out the window
of my truck as I drove at least well
past the speed limit and I coughed
and coughed and spit and spit until
there was nothing left and I sat there
wondering what the fuck was I so
anxious about.

I send my poems and plays out
to the masses and the rejection
outweighs the acceptance and I like
to believe it is because I am too far
ahead of those who choose good

from bad and so I continue to
grind out poems and plays and
I keep sending them out and keep
getting rejected and so as I write
more and more and I know one day
they will see something in my work
and as they lay me into the ground
they will ask me for one more poem
but it will be too late as the
last poem will be coming
with me.

as the evening came at us
I said I love you to my two
youngest kids and me and the dog
got upon my king size bed and she took
her side and I took mine as two fans
blew hot air on us as the dog had an
itch and she chewed away whatever
it was biting her and I closed my eyes
and relived the day and it was ok as
I hugged one of my pillows and began
to dream of that young lady and how
she had given me a piece of her
as the dog and I
began
to
snore.

The scent of discovery

we were so young when we
met and we both wanted to
be famous and she was and I went
into a shell of a man and all I had left
were morsels of our love making and
how we used to mock the world and as
she walked upon the stage I would sit at the back
and revel in her brilliance.

I left and she stayed and I drove
my beat up car out west and into
a snow storm and my car died as the
ice from the heavens fell and engulfed
me and I near froze to death but I still
had those images of our heated love making
and it kept me warm until the sun came up
and I walked back to town and stayed a
couple of nights in a seedy motel until my
car had thawed out and I was on my way
west where I thought I would
start all over with my broken
heart in my pocket.

today we both have three kids
and she is happy and I am too as
I write poems about her and how
we used to dance around everyone
else and we would love and hate
each other and she would leave
and always come back and I would
accept her and we kissed and cried
and laughed at everyone else as we

tormented each other in our love
making and then she would leave
again and come back and that was the
way it had to be I guess.

this will not be the last poem
for her as I am sure she never
reads my work and that too is ok
because for me to release her and bring
her back gives to me control for
once in my life and with these few
lines I say to her:
I love you
and
please
do
not
come
back.

Created

we come from the sky and we
have been here in this village
forever and we are those who
fish the river and we are as
humble as they come and we
teach our children right from
wrong but still we falter as we all
liked to drink and smoke
and that lessened our numbers
by quite a bit but today I am sober
and I am free of all poisons but
our kids walk out of this village
and they fall into traps and we welcome
them back and tell them to be safe and we
can only pray that they do.

it is glorious here on this island
and when I look out my window
I can see the river as it rises and drops
and flows and flows and I can tell the
seasons by the flow of the river and I can
tell that the summer fish are returning
to their home up into the mountains where
they will die and a new breed of fish will
be born and they will eat for four years
and they will do it all over as I look out
my window as I have for centuries.

I scratch and scratch as the mosquitoes
are feeding on us and your body gets
used to it after weeks of torment and
all I do is itch and scratch the itch as if I am

being punished for my sins and I accept this
and pay my dues in a quart of blood as the
last mosquito bites at my brown skin and I fade
a little as I scratch my arms as if I am being
punished.

we came from the sky and we fell right
here and we only move when we chase
the fish and we live here with our children
and they will live here with their children
and so on as the river flows and the
seasons change and when it is all over
for me they will put me in a cedar box
and put me in a cedar tree and the
mosquitoes will come and visit but there
will be nothing left of me to feed them
as the river stops for a moment
as
summer
becomes
the
fall.

Outdone by his stories

I was in my first fight at the
age of four and I took a good beating
as some white boys did not like my
brown skin and so I waited for them
to get off the school bus and I chased them
down and swung a hockey stick at them
as tears were rolling down my face as my
mother yelled for me to stop but I kept
swinging and from that day forward I knew
I was an Indian and my skin was a bother to
those who thought they were better than me
and they were as they ran home all with
bruises on their arms and legs and when
I stopped swinging I walked back home
to get the beating I knew
I would get from my father.

in high school I would fight with anyone
and some I won but most I lost and it gave
me peace of mind as I bled from a torn lip
or a cut eye and all would come and cheer
us on as the blood fest was the highlight
of the day and I kept fighting until I dropped
out of school and never was a legend but I knew
from that moment on that I would probably
fight until I die.

later I was hired to fight in clubs and I trained
every day because I knew that if I got caught
and pounded out I would be out of a job so
every fight I destroyed the other man and threw
them out the door and unto the street and I was

doing ok until I fought a biker from a well known
club and I kicked the shit out
of him but in the end I realized
that dying for ten bucks an hour
was not worth it.

today I do not fight anymore as
I walk away in hope that I will not
ever have to fight unless my kids
are threatened or I am threatened
then I will go for it but these days
I am no longer in any situations that
can lead to a fight so I guess I am at peace
with this violent world we live in and I sit
back and watch the wars go on and I wonder
if I would ever raise a hand to another human
but I do not as my mother screams for me
to stop
and I did
mom
I
did
stop.

Whisper from you

the heat is causing all of us
to consider murder but we never do
we just sweat it out and when the night
finally falls you relish the coolness and
you settle down for the dreams to come
and they do and I had a dream about being
in love with many women at one time and it
worked and I knew this was a dream because
in my real life I am still searching for a
heart of gold.

when I wake up each morning I get dressed
in the clothes I have been wearing for a week
now and the dog looks at me in disgust as
even she cleans herself constantly and I put
on a hat I have worn every day for over a year
now to hide all of my vanity as if there
will be a princess out there
for me and I reheat a coffee from
the day before and I light a cigarette
and the routine is set and I walk out
and get in my truck and I drive down
the dirt road and across the bridge
and I am in a new world and it is one
that takes and takes and I give and give
and I buy a fresh cup of coffee and I light
a cigarette and people stare at me for a
moment as I fade in and out of focus
because I am not really here or there.

a whisper from you gives to me
the strength to keep going and I do
as I drive back down across the bridge

and down the dirt road and the dog barks
at me as if I had been gone for a century
and I sit down at my desk and I break out
a book of poems and I write one more
poem to finish a new book and it comes
so easily and so I send it out to be rejected
and it is rejected and one ass of an editor
told me I should add some imagery to my work
and I am not even sure what that means
but I took it he did not like my work so fuck
him and all those who reject because this
old poet is going to light a cigarette
take a sip of cold coffee
tie his shoes he has worn for a year
scratch his head
and stare at the dog
as she
licks herself
clean.

About the Author

Joseph A. Dandurand is a member of Kwantlen First Nation located on the Fraser River about 20 minutes east of Vancouver. He resides there with his three children – Danessa, Marlysse, and Jace. Joseph is the Director of the Kwantlen Cultural Centre. He received a Diploma in Performing Arts from Algonquin College and studied Theatre and Direction at the University of Ottawa. He is the author of 12 poetry collections including: *The Rumour* (2018), *I Want* (2015) and *Hear And Foretell* (2015) and *SH:LAM* (2019).